DINOSAUR WORLDS

DINOSAUR GIANTS

Don Lessem

Heinemann

DINOSAUR WORLDS: DINOSAUR GIANTS
was produced by Bender Richardson White, Uxbridge, UK.

Editors: Lionel Bender, Andy Boyles
Designer: Ben White
Editorial Assistants: John Stidworthy, Madeleine Samuel
Picture Researchers: Lionel Bender, Don Lessem
Media Conversion and Typesetting:
 Peter MacDonald and Diacritic
Production: Kim Richardson
Senior Scientific Consultant: Dr Peter Dodson, Professor of
Anatomy and Geology at the University of Pennsylvania
School of Veterinary Medicine, and Vice-President of the
Dinosaur Society.

First published in the USA in 1996 by
Highlights for Children, Honesdale, Pennsylvania 18431.

This edition published in Great Britain in 1996
by Heinemann Children's Reference, an imprint
of Heinemann Educational Publishers, a division of Reed
Educational and Professional Publishing Limited,
Halley Court, Jordan Hill, Oxford OX2 8EJ.

MADRID ATHENS
FLORENCE PRAGUE WARSAW
PORTSMOUTH NH CHICAGO SAO PAULO MEXICO
SINGAPORE TOKYO MELBOURNE AUCKLAND
IBADAN GABORONE JOHANNESBURG KAMPALA NAIROBI

© 1996 Highlights for Children, USA

ISBN 0 431 05659 5 Hb   ISBN 0 431 05662 5 Pb

British Library Cataloguing-in-Publication Data.
A catalogue record for this book is available
from the British Library.

Printed in Spain

**This book is recommended by the Dinosaur Society UK.
For more information please contact The Dinosaur Society UK,
P O Box 329, Canterbury, Kent, CT4 5GB**

Acknowledgments
Photographs Pages: 5: Mark A. Philbrick/Brigham Young University.
10: V. R. Hammer, Augustana College. 15: Tom Leach/Oxford
Scientific Films. 16, 17: V. R. Hammer. 20: The Natural History
Museum, London. 24: Breck P. Kent/Oxford Scientific Films.
26 – 27 and 27 (inset): The Natural History Museum, London.
31: Mark A. Philbrick/Brigham Young University. 33: Dr Jeremy
Burgess/Oxford Scientific Films. 34–35: Anthony Bannister/Natural
History Photo Agency. 37: Dr David Gillette, Division of Antiquities,
Salt Lake City. 40 and 43: Dr Gunther Viohl, Jura Museum, Eichstätt.
44-45: Trevor McDonald/Natural History Photo Agency. 46: The Natural History
Museum, London.
Illustrations All major double-page scenes by Steve Kirk. All other
major illustrations by James Field. Ecology diagrams and small
featured creatures by Jim Robins. Step-by-step sequences by John
James. Maps by Ron Hayward. Cover illustration by Steve Kirk.

GLOSSARY

The Jurassic Period lasted from 208 million to 145 million years ago. In the Jurassic Period, dinosaurs were often not the most common vertebrates. Other less familiar animals included:

Cynodonts (SY-no-donts) Mammal-like reptiles with dog-like teeth. They lived from before the Triassic to well into the Jurassic Period. They were direct ancestors of mammals.

Ichthyosaurs (ICK-thee-o-saws) Fish-shaped, air-breathing marine reptiles that ate fish.

Invertebrates (in-VER-teh-braits) Animals without backbones. Marine invertebrates, such as ammonites, are well preserved among other fossils of the Late Jurassic.

Labyrinthodonts (LAB-uh-RIN-tho-donts) Fat-bodied amphibians of many forms and sizes, most of which had a pattern like a maze, or labyrinth, inside their teeth.

Mammals (MAM-uls) Animals with hair that nurse their young. Mammals were present throughout the age of dinosaurs, although during that time they never grew larger than domestic cats.

Pterodactyls (TAIR-o-DACK-tills) Pterosaurs with long necks and short tails that grew both small and large in the Jurassic Period and in the following Cretaceous Period.

Pterosaurs (TAIR-o-SAWS) Flying reptiles, the first backboned animals to fly.

Rhamphorhynchids (RAM-fo-RING-kids) Small Jurassic pterosaurs with lightweight skulls and long tails with diamond-shaped flaps.

Tritylodontids (try-TIE-lo-DON-tids) Mammal-like reptiles that grew to the size of beavers in the Early Jurassic Period.

ECOLOGICAL TERMS

atmosphere the layer of gases that surrounds the Earth; also known as the air.

carnivore a meat-eating animal.

climate the average weather conditions in a particular part of the world.

continent a huge area of land on Earth, such as North America, South America, Europe and Australia.

environment the total living conditions, including landscape, climate, plants and animals.

evolved changed, over many generations, to produce a new species, body feature or way of life.

geography the study of the Earth and all of its features, such as its mountains, oceans, weather, life (both plants and animals), and human activity.

geology the study of the materials of the Earth's rocks, minerals and fossils and the processes by which they are formed.

habitat the local area in which an animal or plant lives, for example, a desert, forest or lake.

herbivore a plant-eating animal.

migrate to move from place to place as conditions change or to reproduce.

predator a meat-eating animal that hunts and kills.

prey an animal that is hunted and eaten by a predator.

scavenger a meat-eating animal that does not make its own kills but eats the bodies of animals already dead.

species a group of living things in which individuals look alike and can reproduce with one another.

vegetation plant life.

ABOUT THIS BOOK

Welcome to *Dinosaur Worlds*. In these pages you will see dinosaurs as you have never seen them before – with their fellow animals and plants in the environments they inhabited. Dinosaurs were a highly successful and varied group of land reptiles with fully upright postures and S-curved necks that lived from 228 million to 65 million years ago.

Dinosaur Giants explores the environments of the dinosaurs in the Jurassic Period, from 208 to 145 million years ago, and traces the dinosaurs' success in a time of great changes. During this period, dinosaurs grew to sizes far greater than other animals have ever reached. It reveals these giants' worlds as today's leading scientists and artists see them, based on fossil records. Fossils are the remains of once-living creatures that have been preserved in rocks. Comparisons with living animals and habitats help to fill in details that fossils cannot provide.

This book is divided into four chapters, each looking at a specific dinosaur fossil site and revealing a different feature of dinosaur life and death. A short introductory section provides background information about the world at this time. It also contains a visual explanation of scientific and technical terms used in the book.

Enjoy your journey of discovery to the lost worlds of the dinosaurs!

"Dino" Don. Lessem

Measurements
This book uses metric units of measure:
centimetre (cm) , metre (m),
kilogram (kilo) and tonne
1 cm = 0.4 inch, 1m = 40 inches = 3.3 feet
1 kilo = 2.2 pounds
1 tonne (1,000 kilos) is approximately 1 ton

CONTENTS

Within each chapter of the book are five double-page spreads. The first spread is a large, dramatic scene at the site millions of years ago. The second spread, 'A Look Back In Time', identifies and describes the major animals and plants in the scene and highlights the environment. The next spread, 'Featured Creatures', gives basic facts and figures about the most interesting animals and plants. Spread four, 'Then And Now', compares dinosaurs and their worlds with present-day animals and habitats. The last spread in each chapter, 'How Do We Know?', looks at the scientific evidence for all this – the fossils and what they reveal about the behaviour and ecology of dinosaurs.

JURASSIC LANDSCAPE

The Jurassic Period, from 208 million to 145 million years ago, was the central time in dinosaur evolution. During this span of 62 million years, dinosaurs became the dominant animals on Earth. By the Late Jurassic, some plant-eating dinosaurs, the brachiosaurs, grew bigger than any other land animals before them. Flying reptiles (pterosaurs) and sea reptiles (such as ichthyosaurs and plesiosaurs) evolved into many new forms. The first butterflies, moths and birds appeared in the Jurassic. Small mammals lived in the shadows of the giant dinosaurs.

FOSSIL FINDS AROUND THE WORLD

The map shows the present-day continents and the dinosaur fossil sites from the Jurassic Period. The four sites featured in this book are shown in red. The most famous of all Jurassic dinosaurs are the giant plant-eaters, the sauropods.

Early Jurassic dinosaurs lived on many continents. Prosauropod dinosaurs - forerunners of the sauropods - and new predatory dinosaurs spread across the globe, even to **Antarctica**. At the time, Antarctica was not frozen, but cool and moist.

CLIMATE

In the Jurassic, the climate varied in different parts of the world. Early on, the Jurassic Period was wetter than the Triassic (245 million to 208 million years ago), but later the inland areas became dry again.

CONTINENTS

The shape of the land changed greatly in the Jurassic Period. The single land mass, Pangaea, which existed in the Triassic, began to break up. The northern part, Laurasia, moved away from the southern part, named Gondwana. A shallow but gradually widening sea formed between the supercontinents of Laurasia and Gondwana.

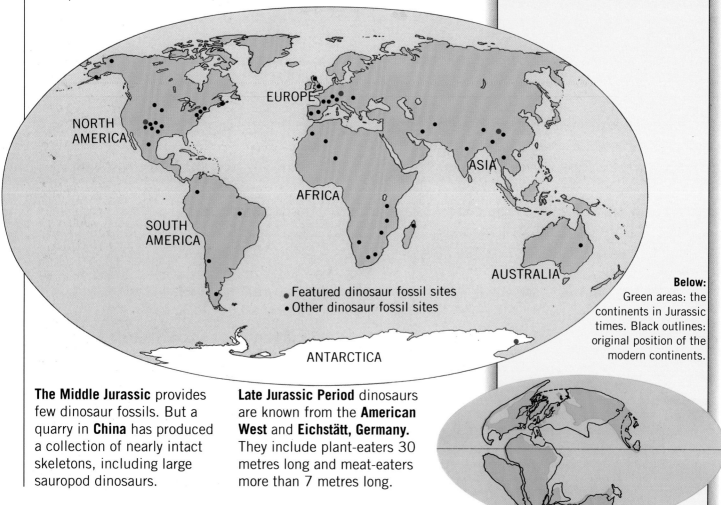

EUROPE

NORTH AMERICA

ASIA

AFRICA

SOUTH AMERICA

AUSTRALIA

• Featured dinosaur fossil sites
• Other dinosaur fossil sites

ANTARCTICA

Below:
Green areas: the continents in Jurassic times. Black outlines: original position of the modern continents.

The Middle Jurassic provides few dinosaur fossils. But a quarry in **China** has produced a collection of nearly intact skeletons, including large sauropod dinosaurs.

Late Jurassic Period dinosaurs are known from the **American West** and **Eichstätt, Germany.** They include plant-eaters 30 metres long and meat-eaters more than 7 metres long.

In much of the world, the climate of the Jurassic Period was dry. Lowland valleys were the wettest places and had the thickest vegetation. Many of the plants were similar to those of the Triassic Period. Ferns were common in the clearings. Cycads and related plants, such as the bennettitaleans, grew as shrubs and low-growing plants. New kinds of trees included a deciduous tree related to the conifers, and the ginkgo, which is still alive today. (The ginkgo is a native plant of China.)

The sky was filling with life. The many kinds of small, long-tailed rhamphorhynchid pterosaurs still flourished. The shorter-tailed pterodactyls evolved in the Late Jurassic. The first birds arose from dinosaurs in the Jurassic.

New kinds of dinosaurs included stegosaurs, sauropods and *Allosaurus* (see page 16), one of the largest of all carnivores. Bony fishes became more common in the sea. They were preyed upon by marine reptiles such as *Ichthyosaurus* (see page 40).

Fossil explorer "Dino" Jim Jensen puts the finishing touches on a full-sized recreation of the front leg of *Ultrasauros*, a Jurassic giant dinosaur he named. *Ultrasauros* may have reached six storeys in height, making it among the largest of all dinosaurs.

The skeleton of an animal rebuilt from its bones or from casts of the bones is known as a reconstruction.

A JURASSIC DINOSAUR: *Brachiosaurus*

The largest animals of the Jurassic Period were among the biggest creatures ever on Earth. Largest of all these Jurassic giants were the brachiosaurs. These plant-eaters were part of a community of land animals that included smaller plant- and meat-eating dinosaurs, reptiles, mammals and amphibians.

GEOLOGICAL TIME
Dinosaurs lived during the Mesozoic Era, from 245 to 65 million years ago. The Jurassic Period, 208 to 145 million years ago, was the middle Mesozoic.

THE CYCLE OF LIFE
Dinosaurs fitted into the web of life in their environment. Plants were eaten by animals ranging from tiny insects to giant dinosaurs. Plant-eaters were preyed on by carnivores or eaten by scavengers after death. Remains of dead animals and plants, and animal waste, including that from dinosaurs, was broken down by small organisms into soil nutrients. These nutrients fed plants. The plants grew in the rain and sun, providing more food for animals as the cycle of life continued.

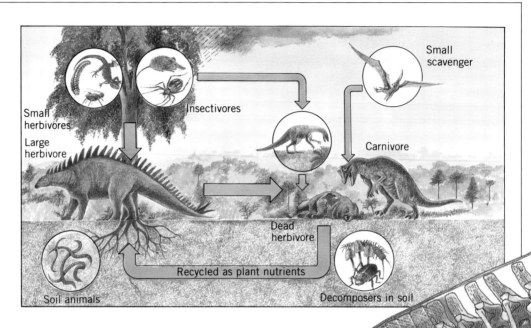

Small herbivores
Insectivores
Small scavenger
Large herbivore
Carnivore
Dead herbivore
Recycled as plant nutrients
Soil animals
Decomposers in soil

TAIL
Although *Brachiosaurus* is often shown with its tail on the ground, we have no evidence to suggest that it dragged its tail. In fact *Brachiosaurus* had thick tail muscles that could have kept the tail aloft. *Brachiosaurus* had a short tail compared to some other sauropods. It had about fifty tail vertebrae.

SKIN
No skin impressions of *Brachiosaurus* are known, so the texture and pattern of its skin are a mystery. But other sauropod dinosaur skin impressions have been found, showing a pattern of tiny bumps, called tubercles, across the scaly skin. It is likely that *Brachiosaurus* had similar skin. No one knows the colours of any dinosaur. Big animals are often drab, but dinosaurs' closest relatives, birds, are highly colourful.

ANATOMY OF A DINOSAUR

Brachiosaurus is one of the biggest dinosaurs known from a nearly complete skeleton, which was actually made from several partial *Brachiosaurus* skeletons. At the time of the discovery of *Brachiosaurus* one hundred years ago, many scientists thought the giant sauropods were too heavy to have stood on land, and so must have spent most of their time in the water. But it was not until the 1970s that palaeontologists agreed that *Brachiosaurus* was a land-dwelling dinosaur that fed from the trees.

SKULL
Brachiosaurus's skull and the brain cavity within it were small in comparison to its huge body. The teeth were large and shaped like chisels. They show heavy wear marks indicating they bit into tough plant fibres. *Brachiosaurus* had huge nostrils. Scientists can only guess whether these big openings were designed for a keen sense of smell, for making noise or for cooling the animal.

CHEST RIBS
Brachiosaurus weighed more than 50 tonnes. It would have been heavier still without several weight-saving features in its skeleton. For instance, the ribs in its chest were hollow, as were the neck vertebrae. Large air spaces separated by thin sheets of bone were features of the rear backbones, or vertebrae.

FRONT LEGS
Brachiosaurus means 'arm reptile'. It was named for the length of its front legs compared with its hind legs. The front leg bones and shoulder bones of *Brachiosaurus* stood 4.5 metres high.

MUSCLES
Muscles of *Brachiosaurus* and other dinosaurs are not preserved. The sizes of muscles are indicated by the grooves in bones where those muscles attached.

FOOT
Brachiosaurus had four or five short toes, spread wide to support its immense weight.

LIFESTYLE
How did *Brachiosaurus* get its food? Its build suggests it fed from high in the trees, for *Brachiosaurus* stood more than 13 metres high with its head raised. Whether it could hold its head high for a long time without becoming dizzy is uncertain. The pressure required to pump blood to a head held so high would be enormous.

Brachiosaurus had a horse-sized head, but its body was more than fifty times the size of a horse. It is unlikely that it could have chewed thoroughly all the food it needed. Instead, much of the breakup of food probably happened in its stomach. The stomach was a huge vat, where small rocks (gastroliths) that the animal had swallowed helped grind food so that digestion could take place (see page 37).

Brachiosaurus's diet was low-energy plants. How did it get enough energy to keep its huge body going? Its great size and the warm climate might have helped its temperature stay high without burning much energy to stay warm. Nor did *Brachiosaurus* need to rush about. Perhaps its energy needs were relatively low.

SOUTHERN JUNGLE
MT. KIRKPATRICK
Antarctica

200 million years ago

The sun rises over a seashore beside a forest of conifers swathed in mist. Meat-eating dinosaurs share a feast in the waves while a bigger carnivore approaches.

ANTARCTIC JUNGLE

Dinosaurs lived on every continent, including what is now Antarctica. During the Early Jurassic, Antarctica was further north than it is today, and it had warm, moist weather. The bones of dinosaurs found in the frozen mountains of Antarctica offer new clues about the appearance and behaviour of predatory dinosaurs.

In 1991, scientists exploring 650 kilometres from the South Pole discovered the remains of a large and unfamiliar meat-eating dinosaur in rocks from this time. This carnivore, which has been named *Cryolophosaurus*, was remarkable because of the unusual crest on its head. It might have been the Early Jurassic's biggest meat-eater. Two other dinosaurs were also found on Antarctica. The first resembled *Coelophysis*, a smaller carnivore that lived in western North America. The second seemed to be related to *Dilophosaurus*, another Early Jurassic meat-eater of western North America.

CRYOLOPHOSAURUS

DILOPHOSAURUS

Mount Kirkpatrick – Today The Antarctic is colder than a deep freeze, even in summer. On the slopes of this mountain, geologists found dinosaur bones.

In the Early Jurassic, predatory dinosaurs evolved into larger and more elaborate forms. The crests of *Cryolophosaurus* and *Dilophosaurus* might have served as displays used to attract mates or frighten rivals. As in modern animals, it might have been that only male dinosaurs had these display features. Crests could also have frightened enemies.

FACT FILE

ANIMALS
1. Ammonites (AM-uh-nights)
2. *Coelophysis*-like carnivore
   (SEE-lo-FY-sis)
3. *Cryolophosaurus*
   (CRY-o-LO-fo-SAW-rus)
4. *Nautilus* (NOUGT-ih-lus)
5. Rhamphorhynchid
   (RAM-fo-RING-kid)

PLANTS
6. *Brachyphyllum* conifer
   (BRACK-ee-FILL-um)
7. Podocarp conifer
   (POE-doe-karp)

ALSO AT THIS SITE:
Dilophosaurus-like carnivore
   (die-LO-fo-SAW-rus)
Oreochima fish
   (ORE-ee-o-KY-mer)
Prosauropod plant-eater
   (pro-SAW-ro-pod)
Tritylodont (try-TIE-lo-DONT)
Seed ferns

Mount Kirkpatrick – Then The dawn light is misty and dim in a coastal forest. It is early in the Jurassic, the first period in which the largest plant- and meat-eaters on land were dinosaurs.

Between the sea and the forest, *Cryolophosaurus*, a 7.5-metre-long predatory dinosaur, searches for its next meal. Behind this killer, the forest is home to such animals as tritylodonts – mammal-like reptiles the size of a beaver – that might make a meal. In front of *Cryolophosaurus*, one of its own kind is being eaten in the shallows by a *Coelophysis*-like dinosaur and its young. Overhead, a pterosaur, the size of a crow, flaps towards the water.

It looks down at a school of *Oreochima* (see page 13).

COELOPHYSIS

Not all predatory dinosaurs had crests. *Coelophysis* might have used changing skin-colour patterns to communicate during courtship displays. Some dinosaurs might have communicated with calls.

Antarctica, Then and Now
About 200 million years ago Antarctica was the most southerly part of the world, just as it is today. But then it was still part of the world's single continent and much closer to the equator.

Mt. Kirkpatrick

Globe shows the position of the continents now.

NEW DISCOVERIES IN THE ICE

Because dinosaur remains had been found all over the world, scientists believed that dinosaurs must have lived in Antarctica, too. But it was not until 1986 that fossil evidence of dinosaurs was discovered there. Among the most dramatic of the discoveries was the accidental find of the meat-eater *Cryolophosaurus*.

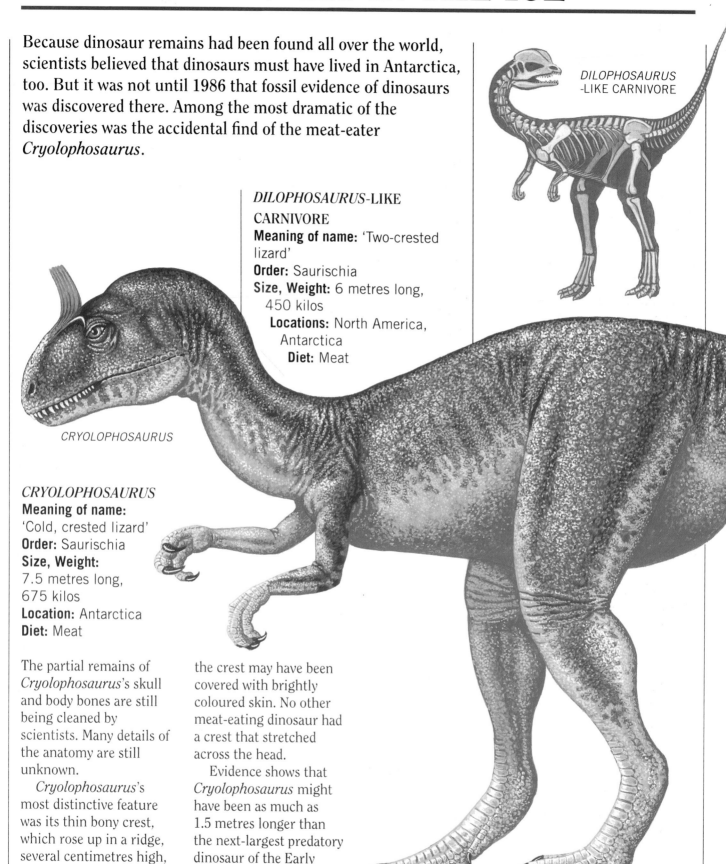

DILOPHOSAURUS -LIKE CARNIVORE

CRYOLOPHOSAURUS

DILOPHOSAURUS-LIKE CARNIVORE
Meaning of name: 'Two-crested lizard'
Order: Saurischia
Size, Weight: 6 metres long, 450 kilos
Locations: North America, Antarctica
Diet: Meat

CRYOLOPHOSAURUS
Meaning of name: 'Cold, crested lizard'
Order: Saurischia
Size, Weight: 7.5 metres long, 675 kilos
Location: Antarctica
Diet: Meat

The partial remains of *Cryolophosaurus*'s skull and body bones are still being cleaned by scientists. Many details of the anatomy are still unknown.

Cryolophosaurus's most distinctive feature was its thin bony crest, which rose up in a ridge, several centimetres high, across its skull. In life, the crest may have been covered with brightly coloured skin. No other meat-eating dinosaur had a crest that stretched across the head.

Evidence shows that *Cryolophosaurus* might have been as much as 1.5 metres longer than the next-largest predatory dinosaur of the Early Jurassic, *Dilophosaurus*.

TRITYLODONT

TRITYLODONT
Meaning of name: 'Three-knobbed tooth'
Order: Therapsida
Size, Weight: 1.2 metres long, 13.5 kilos
Locations: England, western North America, China, South Africa, Antarctica
Diet: Plants

Tritylodonts were mammal-like reptiles with unusual teeth. They had large fangs in the front of their jaws with a toothless gap on either side. At the back of the jaws were seven square 'cheek' teeth on each side. Each upper tooth had three knobs. Lower teeth had two knobs. Tritylodonts ground up plants by sliding their lower jaws back and forth.

OREOCHIMA
Meaning of name: 'Mountain winter storm'
Order: Teleostei
Size, Weight: 2.5 centimetres long, 30 grams or less
Location: Antarctica
Diet: Aquatic plants and insects

This fossil fish was found on an Antarctic mountain during a winter blizzard - hence its name.

OREOCHIMA

Worldwide, during the Late Triassic and the Early Jurassic Periods, many new creatures inhabited the sea as well as the air and land. Along with giant sea reptiles and the first turtles, new kinds of fish lived at this time.

The teleosts became one of the most successful groups of fish. They evolved in the Late Triassic Period 220 million years ago. By the end of dinosaur time, 65 million years ago, they had become the most common bony fishes in the world. They still are. They began as small fish resembling herring. These early teleosts had flexible upper and lower jaws, and upper and lower tail fins that were similar in shape.

PLANTS

The plant life of Antarctica in the Early Jurassic is not well known. Scientists think that it was like that of the rest of the world. On other lands, there were forests of evergreen trees, such as *Brachyphyllum* conifers. These grew tall, with small needle leaves on their branches. Seed ferns and palm-like cycads were also common. The cycad *Antarcticycas* had 2.5-centimetre-thick stems spreading along the ground, and upright fronds.

CONIFER TREE
and PALM-LIKE CYCADS

FISHING AS A WAY OF LIFE

Two hundred million years ago in what is now Antarctica, forests by the coast would have been damp, sometimes cool, but never freezing. In many ways they were like the rainforests of the American Northwest today. And as in modern temperate rainforests, the big trees in the forests of Early Jurassic Antarctica were conifers.

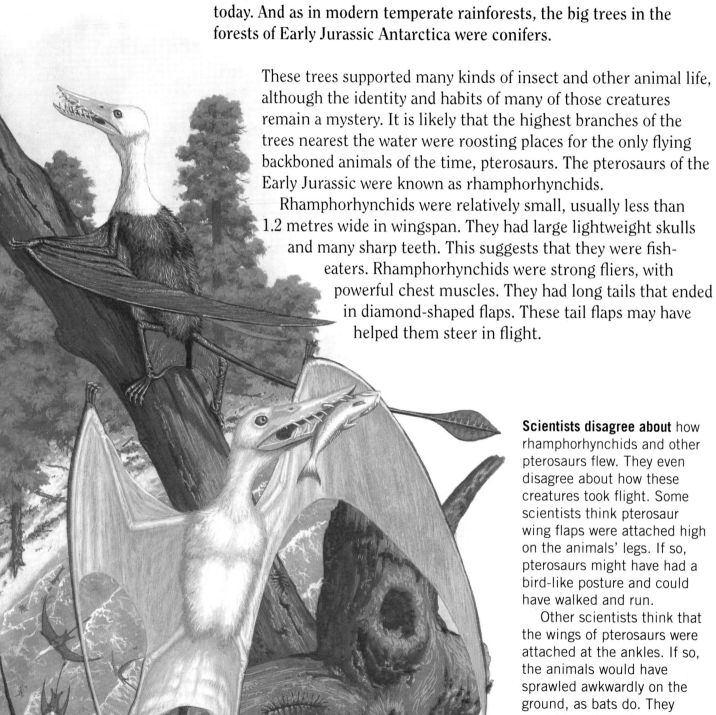

These trees supported many kinds of insect and other animal life, although the identity and habits of many of those creatures remain a mystery. It is likely that the highest branches of the trees nearest the water were roosting places for the only flying backboned animals of the time, pterosaurs. The pterosaurs of the Early Jurassic were known as rhamphorhynchids.
Rhamphorhynchids were relatively small, usually less than 1.2 metres wide in wingspan. They had large lightweight skulls and many sharp teeth. This suggests that they were fish-eaters. Rhamphorhynchids were strong fliers, with powerful chest muscles. They had long tails that ended in diamond-shaped flaps. These tail flaps may have helped them steer in flight.

Scientists disagree about how rhamphorhynchids and other pterosaurs flew. They even disagree about how these creatures took flight. Some scientists think pterosaur wing flaps were attached high on the animals' legs. If so, pterosaurs might have had a bird-like posture and could have walked and run.

Other scientists think that the wings of pterosaurs were attached at the ankles. If so, the animals would have sprawled awkwardly on the ground, as bats do. They would have launched themselves from tree branches or cliffs.

Today, forests offer homes for life at many heights, or levels. Some creatures live on the dark forest floor. Others thrive in the canopy of the leafy treetops. A few creatures live higher still, where the sunny tops of the tallest trees poke out of the forest canopy.

Scientists think that creatures in the evergreen forests of Early Jurassic Antarctica also lived at many levels. On the ground and among the low-growing cycads, amphibians and lizards scurried, preying upon insects and one another. Mammal-like reptiles might have lived in the branches of cycads and taller tree ferns. Near the water, in the tops of towering conifer trees, pterosaurs roosted.

The modern counterparts of the small pterosaurs in Early Jurassic Antarctica may be the ospreys and pelicans of North American lakes and coastal forests. Pterosaurs used their strong chest muscles to flap their broad wings, as do present-day ospreys. Like these birds, pterosaurs might have roosted and nested high in trees.

Two *Cryolophosaurus* (1) hunt in a clearing by a stream where thirsty herbivores are likely to gather. High above the trees **(2)** of this Early Jurassic forest pterosaurs **(3)** look for roosts. Carnivores rely on herbivores for their food. Meat-eaters do not take their energy directly from plants. They get it by eating other animals.

A white pelican scoops fish from the water with its beak. Two hundred million years ago, pterosaurs would have fed in a similar way. They might have swooped and dived to pick fish from the water with their beaks.

BONES FROM THE FREEZER

American researcher Dr William Hammer and his colleagues spent three Antarctic summers excavating fossils on the cold and windy slopes of Mount Kirkpatrick. They found parts of the skull and limbs of *Cryolophosaurus*, teeth of a small meat-eating dinosaur, remains of a large prosauropod dinosaur, a *Dilophosaurus*-like dinosaur and a tritylodont (see pages 12 and 13).

The idea that dinosaurs like *Cryolophosaurus* and *Dilophosaurus* might have used their head crests to communicate comes from observations of many modern animals. Display features that have no other obvious purpose are common among animals today. For example, fiddler crabs have one claw larger than the other and wave it about in ritual courtship dances on the beach. Male deer have large elaborate antlers, which they show off as they raise their heads and call out to win the favour of female deer.

Dr Hammer used a gas-powered saw to penetrate frozen ground and thick, fossil-rich rock in Antarctica. He and the other members of the dig team had their tools flown in by helicopter. Even in summer, they struggled to stay warm as they worked in temperatures of −35 degrees Centigrade.

CREST AND HORNS

In addition to *Cryolophosaurus* and *Dilophosaurus*, several large carnivorous dinosaurs had unusual skulls. *Monolophosaurus* (China, 170 million years ago) had a single crest down the middle of its skull. *Allosaurus* (United States, 145 million years ago) had bony knobs near its eyes. *Carnotaurus* (Argentina, 97 million years ago) had bull-like horns. In addition to using these projections as displays, some of these creatures might have used them in sparring matches with rivals for territory or mates.

Cryolophosaurus

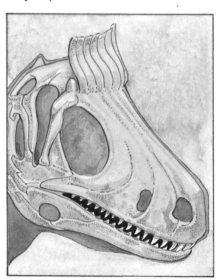

Dilophosaurus

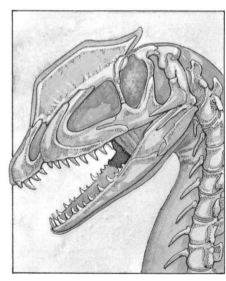

Cryolophosaurus tooth

Modern birds, the closest living relatives of dinosaurs, have many colourful display features and behaviours. For instance, peacocks fan and wave their brilliantly coloured tail feathers as they prance about to draw the attention of peahens. *Cryolophosaurus* may have pushed its head forwards to show off its crest in disputes with rivals over territory, as blue jays do today.

Many living species of reptiles also have colourful displays. Male and female lizards often look very different. This makes it easy for the sexes to recognize each other. Usually the males are more colourful than the females.

Male anole lizards have a flap of skin under the chin that can be expanded in a flash of colour. Male plumed basilisks have colourful crests.

Dr William Hammer, the scientist who found *Cryolophosaurus,* compares its crest to Elvis Presley's haircut, one of the rock musician's own prominent display features. Dr Hammer jokingly calls the dinosaur 'Elvisaurus'.

Monolophosaurus

Allosaurus

Carnotaurus

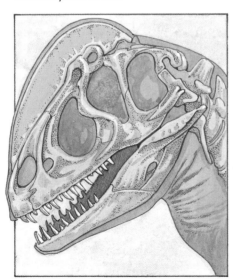

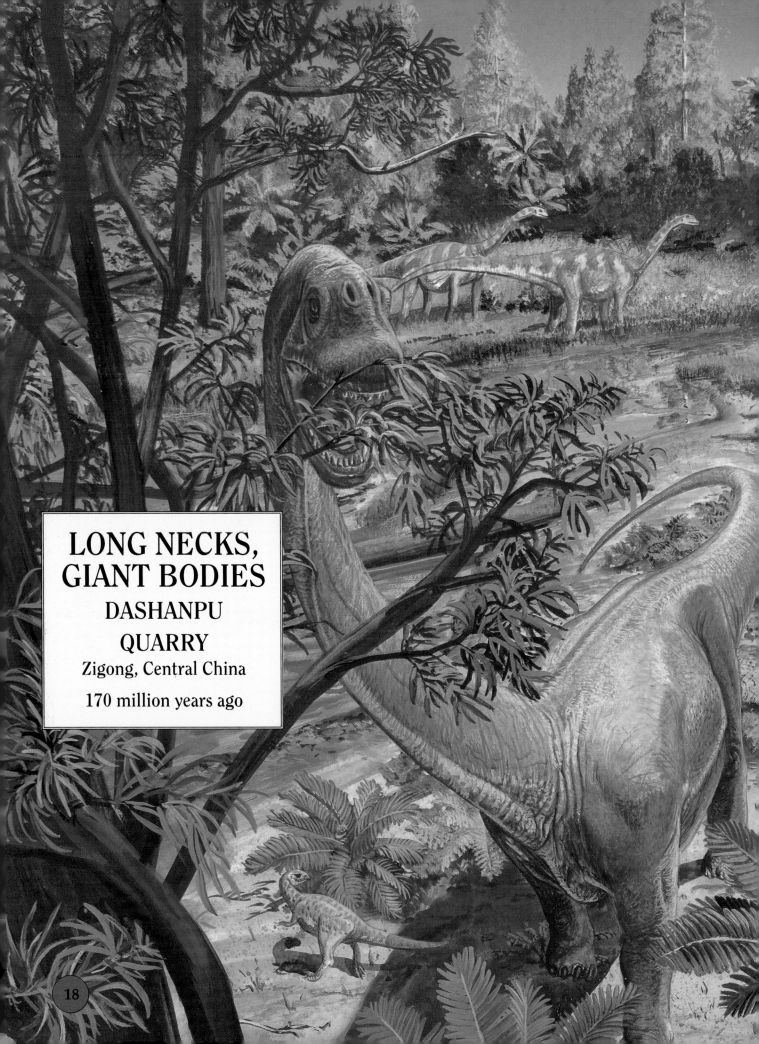

LONG NECKS, GIANT BODIES

DASHANPU QUARRY

Zigong, Central China

170 million years ago

Plant-eating dinosaurs are munching their way through a lush forest amid streams and lakes. Four-legged herbivores, some big, others enormous, feed at different levels of the forest. A pterosaur flies overhead.

CHINESE DINOSAURS

The Middle Jurassic is the mysterious heart of dinosaur time. Around the world, only very few rocks from this time have been found, so dinosaurs and their environments are little known. But in central China, Middle Jurassic plants and animals are preserved in spectacular completeness.

The rock formations here contain entire skeletons of plant-eating dinosaurs as well as fossilized trunks of huge conifer trees. The fossils reveal a hitherto unknown population of large dinosaurs, especially large, four-legged plant-eaters. They lived in a well-watered lowland forest and grew to truly enormous sizes. Some had especially long necks, giving them access to a higher level of the treetops than any other animals had ever reached. The earliest known spike- and plate-backed stegosaurs lived here (see page 23).

Dashanpu Quarry – Today
In the mudstone of Zigong region of Sichuan Province in central China, palaeontologists are digging up some of the world's best-preserved dinosaur fossils.

More than 15 metres long, ***Datousaurus*** was a huge and solidly built early sauropod. Sauropod skulls are rare. But complete *Datousaurus* skulls were found in Dashanpu Quarry.

FEEDING LEVELS

Several different large plant-eaters could share the same environment by feeding at different heights.

Omeisaurus, at more than 17 metres long, was the largest plant-eater in Jurassic China. With its long neck it could stretch to the treetops. At half the height of *Omeisaurus*, *Shunosaurus* could feed from branches well above ground level. *Huayangosaurus* stood low on all fours and could nibble plants on the forest floor.

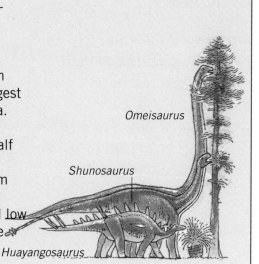

Omeisaurus

Shunosaurus

Huayangosaurus

Dashanpu Quarry – Then

Huge plant-eaters travelled through the forests of central China 170 million years ago. The largest of all, *Omeisaurus*, towered over even the 15-metre-long *Datousaurus* and the 12-metre-long club-tailed *Shunosaurus*. Other plant-eating dinosaurs included spike-backed *Huayangosaurus* (not shown) and the little two-legged *Xiaosaurus*.

Gasosaurus, a long-legged meat-eater 4.5 metres long, is ready to pounce on any animal it can overcome. Above, a big-toothed pterosaur, *Angustinaripterus*, soars in search of fish. An amphibian, a flat-bodied labyrinthodont, lies quietly in the stream. The forest trees are huge evergreen conifers. Seed ferns and cycads grow among the conifers and in forest clearings.

FACT FILE

By the Middle Jurassic dinosaurs had replaced other reptiles as the most important land animals.

China, Then and Now

China is now a part of the vast continent of Asia. During the middle of the Jurassic Period, its land may have been divided into two or more landmasses.

Globe shows the position of the continents now.

Dashanpu Quarry

ANIMALS

1. *Angustinaripterus* (AN-gus-TEEN-ah-RIP-teh-rus)
2. *Gasosaurus* (GAS-o-SAW-rus)
3. Labyrinthodont (LAB-y-RIN-tho-dont)
4. *Omeisaurus* (O-mee-SAW-rus)
5. *Shunosaurus* (SHOO-no-SAW-rus)
6. *Xiaosaurus* (ZHOW-o-SAW-rus)

PLANTS

7. Conifers
8. Cycads
9. Seed ferns

ALSO AT THIS SITE:
Datousaurus (DAT-oo-SAW-rus)
Huayangosaurus (hwi-YANG-o-SAW-rus)

KEEP ON GROWING

The enormous increase in body size shown by the sauropods of Middle Jurassic China was not matched by a similar growth in brain size. These giant dinosaurs, some as long as a tennis court, had brains smaller than table-tennis balls. Small brain size does not necessarily indicate stupidity, but these animals probably were limited in their range of behaviour. They probably spent most of the day walking, feeding and producing waste.

OMEISAURUS

DATOUSAURUS

SHUNOSAURUS

OMEISAURUS
Meaning of name: 'Sacred mountain lizard'
Order: Saurischia
Size, Weight: 16.5 to 20 metres long, up to 20 tonnes
Location: China
Diet: Plants

Omeisaurus was the largest of the sauropods known from Sichuan. Its small skull sat on top of an enormously long and slender neck. The skull had nostrils near the top and teeth shaped like spoons. Most likely, *Omeisaurus* fed from the trees and digested the rough vegetation in its huge stomach vat.

Scientists think that spoon-shaped dinosaur teeth, like those of the sauropods of Middle Jurassic China, were good for cutting tough plants. The pencil-shaped teeth of diplodocids and other, later sauropods (see page 32) were better suited for nipping soft plants, such as those that grew near water. All sauropods had tiny heads and big stomachs. These dinosaurs digested plants with the aid of stones, which they swallowed. The stones helped grind food in their stomachs.

Spoon-shaped tooth

All three of these sauropod dinosaurs lived in Middle Jurassic China, although scientists are not sure that all were present in the same area at the same time. If they did share this habitat, they probably had different food preferences.

PLANTS

Classopolis was a type of conifer that grew 12 metres tall in Jurassic times. Scientists have found pollen grains from this tree among the fossils at Dashanpu Quarry.

CLASSOPOLIS

HUAYANGOSAURUS

SHUNOSAURUS
Meaning of name: 'Lizard from Sichuan' (formerly Shuo)
Order: Saurischia
Size, Weight: 12 metres long, 10 tonnes
Location: China
Diet: Plants

Shunosaurus seems to have been the most common dinosaur in China at this time. It was 'small' – only as long as a removal van. Its remains were very complete. Scientists were surprised to find that it had a club-like tail.

HUAYANGOSAURUS
Meaning of name: 'Lizard from Sichuan' (Huayang = Sichuan)
Order: Ornithischia
Size, Weight: 4 metres long, 1 to 4 tonnes
Location: China
Diet: Plants

Huayangosaurus was an early stegosaur with long spikes. Along its back were pairs of heart-shaped plates. Later stegosaurs featured a double row of spikes on their backs.

DATOUSAURUS
Meaning of name: 'Lizard from Datou'
Order: Saurischia
Size, Weight: 15 metres long, 20 tonnes
Location: China
Diet: Plants

Datousaurus's skeleton suggests it was related to lightly built sauropods like *Diplodocus or Seismosaurus* (see page 32). But its skull is like that of a bulky sauropod, such as *Omeisaurus*.

Since the *Datousaurus* skull and skeleton were found apart, they may come from different kinds of dinosaurs.

23

DEFENCE AGAINST PREDATORS

Plant-eaters' defences against attack included such weapons as horns, spikes and armour in the form of a thick skin. In Middle Jurassic China, *Gasosaurus* and other predators hunted the plant-eating dinosaurs. Among the giant herbivores, only *Shunosaurus* had an obvious weapon – a pineapple-like tail club. By swiping its tail, *Shunosaurus* could give a lethal blow, as a giraffe or kangaroo does with a kick of its leg. The small plant-eaters found in China had either armour or spikes for protection.

In the warm, watery regions of East Africa today, crocodiles are terrifying predators in and near the water. But large plant-eaters like the hippopotamus have defences against these hunters. A full-grown hippopotamus has sharp tusks and big powerful jaws. Snapping its jaws, a hippopotamus can kill a crocodile!

Like the hippopotamus, large plant-eating dinosaurs might have used their size to protect themselves and their young. The young, the old, the small and the weak are the favourite targets of predators because frail and small individuals are the least able to defend themselves. So the meat-eater has the best chance of a successful hunt, with least risk to itself. Yet even lions, the most fearsome of modern predators, fail in their hunting efforts nine times out of ten.

In Middle Jurassic China, some large plant-eaters travelled in herds for protection, helping one another. Later in dinosaur evolution, plant-eaters such as *Iguanodon* were equipped with huge thumb spikes as weapons. *Triceratops* had long horns like those of rhinoceroses today as well as a frill of bone protecting its neck and shoulders.

In the North American wilderness, a young moose stays close to its mother. While the youngster is capable of walking from nearly the moment of birth, it is small and vulnerable to predators such as wolves. By staying close to a healthy and full-sized adult, the young moose has added protection against attack. In a similar way, individual and herding adult sauropods in Middle Jurassic China would have protected their young.

An adult *Huayangosaurus* (1) defends its young against attack from hungry *Gasosaurus* (2). The sharp spikes on the *Huayangosaurus*'s back point towards the predators, and it lashes out with its long-spiked tail. These weapons are not powerful enough to kill a big predator, but they might disable or discourage a hunter from pursuing its prey.

***Huayangosaurus* had spikes** running from its shoulders to the middle of its tail. Its legs were of nearly equal length, whereas later stegosaurs, such as *Stegosaurus*, had shorter forelimbs in proportion to the hind legs (see page 33).

A *Huayangosaurus* and its young feed in the thick foliage around a river. Using their small grinding and nipping teeth, these plant-eaters nibble cycads and ferns growing in forest clearings.

In these clearings the young *Huayangosaurus* are easily visible to predators such as *Gasosaurus*. But the predator will not attack as long as the young dinosaur stays near its parent.

A FANTASTIC FIND

Fossils of land animals of the Middle Jurassic Period are not well known, although *Cetiosaurus*, the first sauropod dinosaur ever discovered, was found in England in Middle Jurassic rocks. But one Chinese site has produced not just a good dinosaur record from this time, but some of the most complete dinosaur fossils ever found. This site was discovered in the early 1960s in Dashanpu, China, by a construction crew. When dinosaurs were discovered, the construction project was halted, and scientists moved in to supervise the excavation.

Chinese palaeontologists uncover dinosaur bones at Dashanpu Quarry (below right). The workers were led by Dr Dong Zhiming of Beijing, China's leading dinosaur scientist. He has excavated more dinosaurs than anyone in history. Dr Dong named Dashanpu's big meat-eater *Gasosaurus* in honour of the gas company that began the excavation.

This spectacular skull of the oldest and most primitive member of the stegosaur family yet found was discovered buried in the ground at Dashanpu Quarry in 1992. Scientists have named the dinosaur *Huayangosaurus*.

Unlike later plated dinosaurs, *Huayangosaurus* had teeth in the front of its jaw (see page 23).

Among the large plant-eating
dinosaurs found in southwestern
China, *Mamenchisaurus* is known
from the Late Jurassic,
Shunosaurus from the Middle
Jurassic and *Yunnanosaurus* from
the Early Jurassic. This region of
China is one of the few on Earth
that preserves dinosaurs from
such a wide range of time – more
than 50 million years.

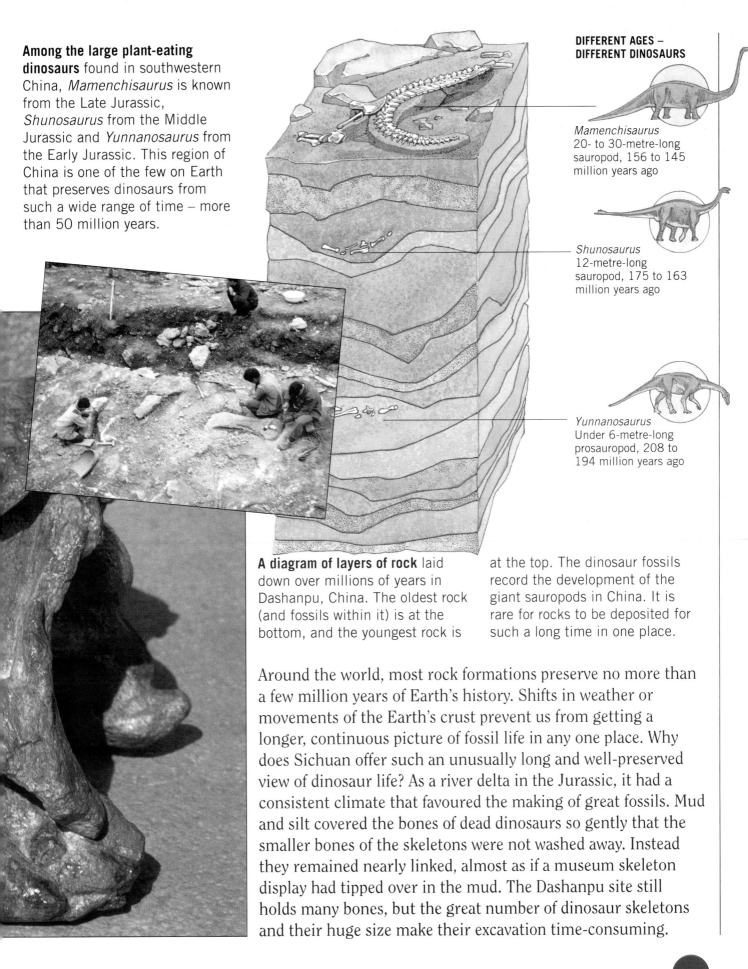

Mamenchisaurus
20- to 30-metre-long
sauropod, 156 to 145
million years ago

Shunosaurus
12-metre-long
sauropod, 175 to 163
million years ago

Yunnanosaurus
Under 6-metre-long
prosauropod, 208 to
194 million years ago

A diagram of layers of rock laid
down over millions of years in
Dashanpu, China. The oldest rock
(and fossils within it) is at the
bottom, and the youngest rock is
at the top. The dinosaur fossils
record the development of the
giant sauropods in China. It is
rare for rocks to be deposited for
such a long time in one place.

Around the world, most rock formations preserve no more than
a few million years of Earth's history. Shifts in weather or
movements of the Earth's crust prevent us from getting a
longer, continuous picture of fossil life in any one place. Why
does Sichuan offer such an unusually long and well-preserved
view of dinosaur life? As a river delta in the Jurassic, it had a
consistent climate that favoured the making of great fossils. Mud
and silt covered the bones of dead dinosaurs so gently that the
smaller bones of the skeletons were not washed away. Instead
they remained nearly linked, almost as if a museum skeleton
display had tipped over in the mud. The Dashanpu site still
holds many bones, but the great number of dinosaur skeletons
and their huge size make their excavation time-consuming.

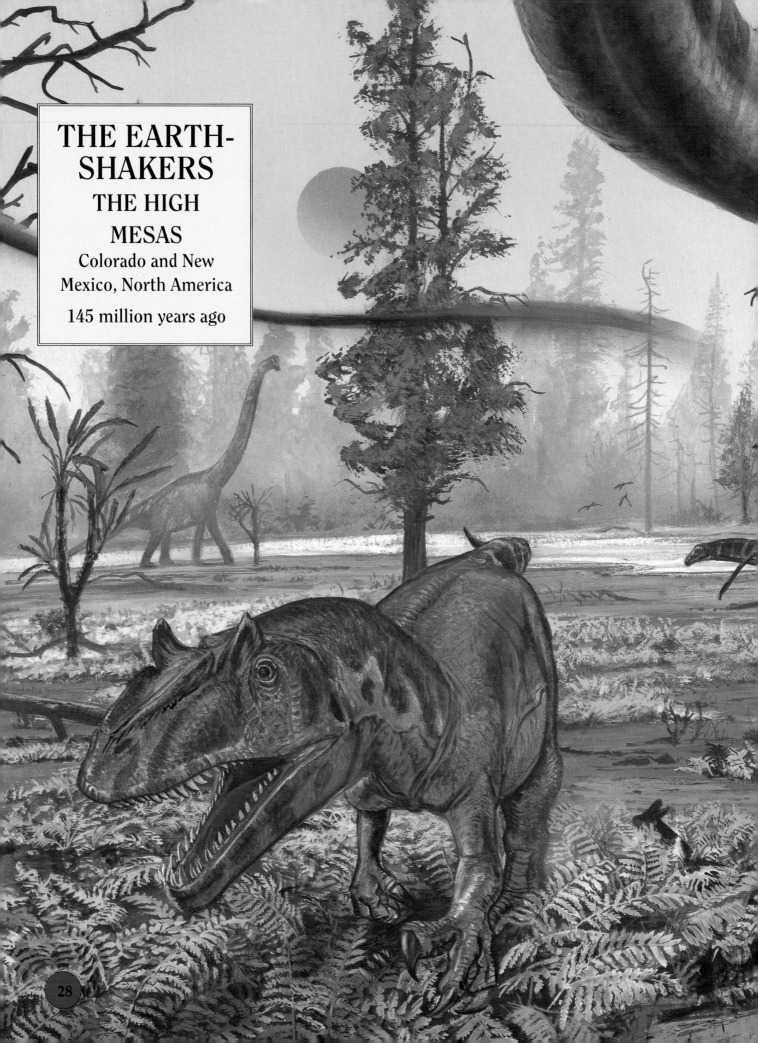

THE EARTH-SHAKERS

THE HIGH MESAS

Colorado and New Mexico, North America

145 million years ago

A warm, dry climate allows the growth of tall conifer trees and low-growing plants. Here, tall dinosaurs live a peaceful life, feeding most of the day. They tower over the smaller dinosaurs, even the large meat-eaters, that roam in their area.

WHY WERE THEY GIANTS?

The ground shook with the footsteps of some of the largest animals ever to walk the Earth – plant-eaters nearly 18 metres tall and more than 30 metres long. The weak and frail among these giant plant-eaters were food for some of the largest of all predatory dinosaurs. As well as the giants, there were many other animals. Small meat-eating dinosaurs preyed on little plant-eating dinosaurs, and other reptiles and small mammals hid in the undergrowth and preyed on one another.

***Nilssonia* was a low-growing cycadeoid plant.** It grew in clearings created by fires, as weeds do today. Many hairy leaves up to a metre long sprouted from its narrow stem.

Its small seeds grew on hair-like stems. The hairs may have discouraged large plant-eaters, but not insects. Many insects like those of today – such as shield bugs, thrips, leaf bugs and plant-hoppers – lived in and around plants like *Nilssonia*.

It is a mystery why Late Jurassic dinosaurs reached sizes never seen before in any land animal. Their environment was not very lush. The climate was warm, but dry. Shallow lakes dotted the forests and clearings. Jurassic trees were neither fast-growing nor packed with foliage. Thick-stemmed cycads and their close relatives, cycadeoids, were some of the most common plants. Their modern relatives have poisonous leaves. Perhaps these Late Jurassic plants were not suitable food for plant-eaters of the *Stegosaurus* type (see page 33), which ate off low-growing vegetation. But clearly, the giant plant-eaters, stretching upwards, found sufficient food among the evergreens.

High Mesas – Today

Supersaurus bones are embedded in rock at Dry Mesa, in western Colorado. The fossil site in this dry region has been excavated for two decades. It has revealed the fossils of two of the largest plant-eaters known, *Supersaurus,* as here, and *Ultrasauros.*

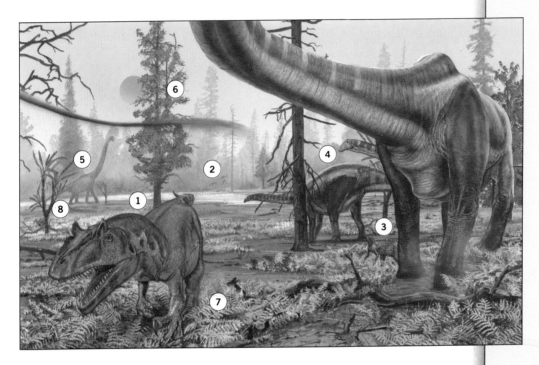

Many giant sauropods are found in western North America, among them the massive brachiosaurs and the lighter diplodocids. Big predators like *Allosaurus* were less common.

ANIMALS
1. *Allosaurus* (AL-o-SAW-rus)
2. *Dermodactylus* (DERM-o-DACK-till-us)
. 3. *Othnielia* (oth-NEE-lee-a)
4. *Seismosaurus* (SIZE-mo-SAW-rus)
5. *Ultrasauros* (UL-tra-SAW-ross)

PLANTS
6. Conifers
7. Ferns
8. *Nilssonia* (nil-SONE-ee-uh)

ALSO AT THIS SITE:
Stegosaurus (STEG-o-SAW-rus)
Supersaurus (SOO-per-SAW-rus)
Cycads
Ginkgoes

Globe shows the position of the continents now.

High Mesas – Then

Near the shore of a shallow lake, where *Nilssonia* plants and ferns spread along the ground, a large *Allosaurus* roars as it moves forwards looking for prey. A small dinosaurian plant-eater, *Othnielia,* looks on. It stands in the shadow of a giant sauropod, a *Seismosaurus,* which sweeps its whip-like tail over the predator.

This and another *Seismosaurus* in front of it are too large to be frightened, even of a 12-metre *Allosaurus.* In the distance, the even bulkier *Ultrasauros* can reach high into the evergreens to nibble and gulp down leaves and twigs. A group of pterosaurs, *Dermodactylus,* fly overhead, looking for fish in the clear water of the lake.

The supergiant dinosaurs of the American West 145 million years ago were part of an animal community in which many smaller dinosaurs prospered. The smallest meat-eaters, like *Ornitholestes,* were less than 2 metres long. The plant-eater *Othnielia,* only 1.5 metres long, ran on slender hind legs.

American West, Then and Now
New Mexico and Colorado were once dry lowlands. Now they are dry but mountainous.

31

HIGH AND HEAVY

ULTRASAUROS

SEISMOSAURUS

The many sauropods of the American West in the Late Jurassic belonged to two groups: the giraffe-necked brachiosaurids and the slimmer, long-tailed diplodocids. Their size is almost beyond belief. Ten bull elephants – the largest modern land animals – might not equal the weight of one of these 'super' sauropods. If *Ultrasauros* were alive today, it could look into the top windows of a six-storey building.

ULTRASAUROS
Meaning of name: 'Beyond lizard'
Order: Saurischia
Size, Weight: 30 metres long, 50 tonnes or more
Location: Colorado
Diet: Plants

Ultrasauros is known from only a few bones of a single animal found in Dry Mesa, Colorado. The best-preserved fossil is a massive 2.7-metre-long shoulder blade. Some scientists think this brachiosaurid might actually be an especially large specimen of *Brachiosaurus*. For years, *Ultrasauros* was considered the largest dinosaur, but it was recently overshadowed by another sauropod found in Argentina.

SEISMOSAURUS
Meaning of name: 'Earth-shaker lizard'
Order: Saurischia
Size, Weight: 30 to 36.5 metres long, 40 tonnes or more
Location: New Mexico
Diet: Plants

Only the back end of a single *Seismosaurus* has been found, but it shows the whole animal must have been more than 30 metres long, making this the longest dinosaur yet found. Its body was slim and had short legs. Since it was a member of the diplodocid family of giant plant-eating dinosaurs, scientists think it had a very long neck that matched its lengthy tail. Some scientists have speculated that the only known specimen may be a particularly large *Diplodocus*.

PLANTS

Plants were slower to change than animals. Many Jurassic plants were similar to those of the Triassic Period. Some remain largely the same today, such as ginkgoes, or maidenhair trees. They are native only to China now, although planted worldwide as ornamental trees. Ginkgoes date back to the Triassic. Their pollen and unique fan-shaped leaves are found in rocks throughout dinosaur time.

Close-up photo of modern ginkgo leaves

DERMODACTYLUS
Meaning of name: 'Skin-finger'
Order: Pterosauria
Size, Weight: 1-metre wingspan, less than 1 kilo
Location: Montana
Diet: Fish

This pterodactyl is known from a wing bone found in 1878.

STEGOSAURUS
Meaning of name: 'Roof lizard'
Order: Ornithischia
Size, Weight: 7.5 metres long, 4 to 7 tonnes
Location: Western North America
Diet: Plants

Stegosaurus was 'bird-hipped' (with a pelvis in which the pubis bone pointed forwards), unrelated to the giant 'lizard-hipped' sauropods (in which the pubis pointed backwards).

Did *Stegosaurus* have one row of plates on its back, or two? This has been a subject of scientists' debates for many decades. *Stegosaurus* was found in the late 1870s in both Wyoming and Colorado. But the most complete discovery, made in Colorado in the early 1990s, revealed that *Stegosaurus* had two rows of pointed plates after all. An as-yet unnamed stegosaur, recently discovered in Utah, had rounder plates on its back.

The function of the plates is also debated. Were they for defence? Were they display features used to frighten predators or to impress mates? Perhaps the best suggestion is that they were body-temperature regulators, since they were full of blood vessels. By positioning the plates towards the morning sun, the stegosaurs could warm themselves. Wind blowing around the plates might have helped cool down an overheated *Stegosaurus*.

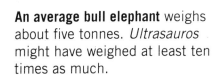

An average bull elephant weighs about five tonnes. *Ultrasauros* might have weighed at least ten times as much.

HERDS ON THE MOVE

The landscape of the American West 145 million years ago was very similar to modern East Africa. Most areas during the Late Jurassic were warm and dry, like the modern African savanna. (But there was none of the savanna's grass in dinosaur times.) Herds of huge plant-eaters moved across the plains and drank from watering holes and shallow lakes, just as elephants, wildebeests and African buffalo do on the savanna now.

In many ways, the lifestyle of these dinosaurs is a mystery. How could they find enough food to eat in a dry environment? In the Late Jurassic, the giant plant-eating dinosaurs probably migrated across the landscape of western North America. By keeping on the move, they found enough food to fuel their enormous bodies, and they would not have stripped the landscape of plant life. If these dinosaurs were not warm-blooded, they would have needed far less food to function than a mammal would at their size. Instead, their bulk and the warm weather would have helped keep their body temperatures high. Moving slowly, they would not have burned much fuel.

As a herd of brachiosaurs travelled, the adults sheltered the young ones by keeping them in the centre of the group, as African elephants do today. Scientists have concluded that herds moved in this way because fossil tracks of a whole herd of these dinosaurs on the move have been found, with small footprints surrounded by larger ones (see pages 6 and 7).

The footprints that the herd made in mud show that the animals were walking slowly. But they may have been able to travel more quickly when the need arose. Some of the meat-eaters, large and small, may have travelled with their prey, just as hyenas follow herds of wildebeest, capturing any that fall behind the herd.

(Photo above) A herd of African elephants migrate. The herd is led by an old female, while the youngsters keep in the centre of the group.

Like the sauropods unearthed in China, North America's giant plant-eaters might have fed on plants at different levels. This split of resources can be seen in present-day African plant-eaters. Giraffes, with their long legs and necks, feed from the trees. Gerenuk antelopes rear on their hind legs to feed from bushes. Zebras, bending their heads down, feed on plants at ground level. The high-shouldered brachiosaurs fed from the treetops at least some of the time. The diplodocids, with their short front legs, probably fed closer to the ground (see page 32).

It may have been hard for diplodocids to keep their giraffe-like necks up for long periods of time. Sometimes, perhaps, they used their necks like the flexible pipe on a vacuum cleaner, allowing their heads to sweep from side to side along the ground or among the vegetation in bushes. Enormous pressure (more than in any living animal) was required to send blood to a head 13 metres in the air. Maybe diplodocids, like giraffes today, had contracting valves in their neck arteries to help pump the blood to their heads.

LIFE OF A GIANT PLANT-EATER

FOOD REQUIREMENTS

Even if *Seismosaurus* (see page 32) and other large dinosaurs were cold-blooded (warmed by their surroundings), they would have had to consume huge amounts of food. An elephant eats around 230 kilos of plant food each day. For a huge dinosaur to take in enough protein for growth and carbohydrates for energy, the animal would have had to eat two or three times as much as this.

How could a dinosaur as large as a block of flats find enough food to survive? How could it mash the food up, with a head only as big as a horse's and with little pencil-shaped teeth? Part of the answer lies in the stones it swallowed to help grind food. A cluster of these stones was found near what had been the stomach of *Seismosaurus*, the longest dinosaur.

Large sauropods could not afford to be fussy eaters. They lived in a dry environment, where plants were not plentiful. Their diet of conifers, cycads, ferns and horsetails was high in fibre but low in nutrients. These dinosaurs probably needed to eat for nearly all their waking hours to meet their energy needs.

1. Digestion was a long process for a sauropod dinosaur. Here a *Seismosaurus* stops to swallow stones. The creature carries them in its stomach to aid digestion. Scientists call stomach stones 'gastroliths'. At times they are rocks made up of minerals that are not typically found where the animal died, evidence that they were carried in the belly of the dinosaur.

2. The *Seismosaurus* reaches a well-watered region with many plants. It reaches out its neck to sweep the area, nipping off many branches with its teeth.

Sauropod teeth were spoon- or pencil-shaped (see page 22) and set in weak-jawed skulls only a metre or two long. Sauropods raked or snipped off plants with their teeth, but must have swallowed their food without chewing.

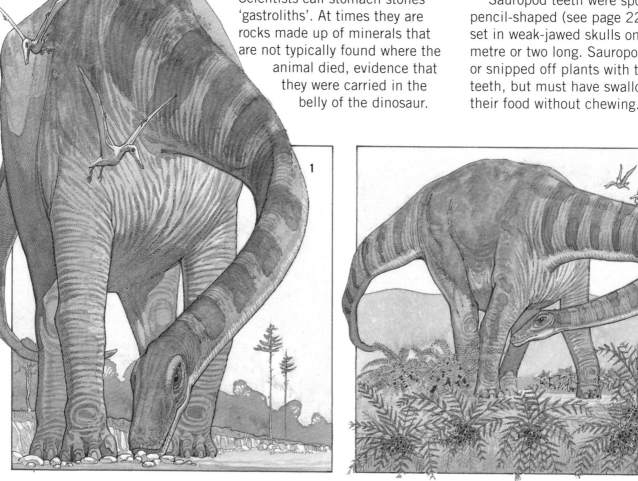

Details of dinosaur digestion are not known, since soft parts of dinosaurs are not preserved. But somewhere in their guts, dinosaurs used stones and acids to break down plants. When *Seismosaurus* was excavated in New Mexico in the 1980s, a pile of gastroliths, or stomach stones, was found in the area that was once the animal's stomach. Perhaps, as in present-day plant-eaters, bacteria in the caecum (a pouch joined to the large intestine) digested the plants further. Finally, undigested material emerged as dung. Fossil dung is known, but none can be definitely identified as having come from sauropods. Most likely, dung was produced in big lumps, like an elephant's.

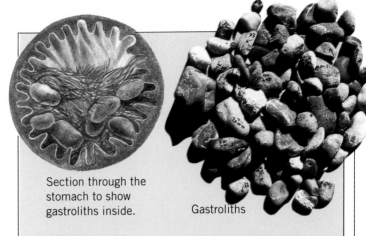

Section through the stomach to show gastroliths inside.

Gastroliths

GASTROLITHS

Gastroliths have a waxy feel and a smooth but finely scratched surface. These are signs of the wear that the stones underwent inside the dinosaur's stomach.

3. In the vast vat that is the animal's stomach, the stones and stomach acid churn about with the plant food. The food breaks into smaller pieces and digestion begins. Some nutrients may be absorbed in the stomach, others in the large intestine. A large proportion of the tough food may not get broken down at all, ending up as waste that gets passed out from the animal.

4. The *Seismosaurus* walks on, feeding and digesting. As food is digested, the animal drops dung. Dung beetles scurry into the waste to deposit their eggs, as they do in elephants' dung today.

Each day, far more than 230 kilos of plant material would have been eaten by a giant sauropod. Hundreds of kilos of dung passed out of the giant, fertilizing the surroundings.

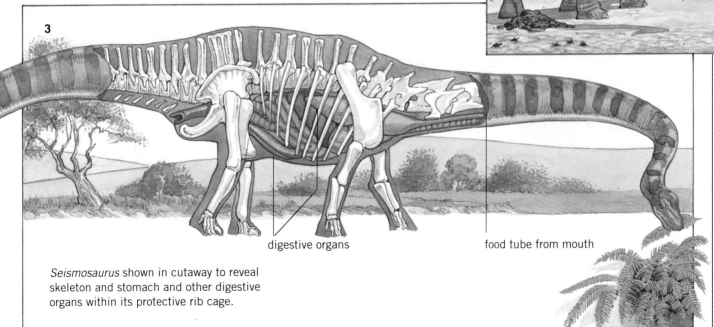

digestive organs

food tube from mouth

Seismosaurus shown in cutaway to reveal skeleton and stomach and other digestive organs within its protective rib cage.

THE POISON LAGOONS
SOLNHOFEN
Eichstätt, Germany
145 million years ago

Under a sub-tropical sky, pterosaurs and a primitive bird soar above a poisoned lagoon. Below, islands formed by coral are homes for plant and animal life.

LIFE IN LAGOONS

In the heart of dinosaur time, Europe was dotted with coral islands and sub-tropical lagoons. Pterosaurs – flying reptiles – glided along the shoreline and dived into the shallow, salty water to catch fish. A few birds flew searching for insects to snatch. On dry land, small dinosaurs hunted lizards. In the water, marine reptiles swam after their prey. Yet in deep lagoon waters at Eichstätt there was no life (see page 44).

Solnhofen Quarry – Today
A stoneworker cuts up a fine-grained block of limestone.
   While splitting the slabs, quarrymen have discovered thousands of spectacularly well preserved fossils. These fossils are the skeletons and impressions of creatures that were buried in the soft bottoms of lagoons 145 million years ago.

During the Late Jurassic, an ichthyosaur glides among coral islands and reefs in search of fish. Also living in these waters are ammonites, horseshoe crabs (see page 47), jellyfish and squid.

The Late Jurassic world had many different habitats and a rich variety of life in the sea and the air, as well as on land. Reptiles dominated oceans and skies as dinosaurs ruled dry land, but there were many other successful animals around.

Several animals we would recognize today – horseshoe crabs, shellfish with coiled, patterned shells, bony fish, squid and jellyfish – lived off the shores of what is now Europe. But the main predators of the ancient seas were creatures now extinct. They included ichthyosaurs, strong-swimming reptiles that resembled modern dolphins in shape and size.

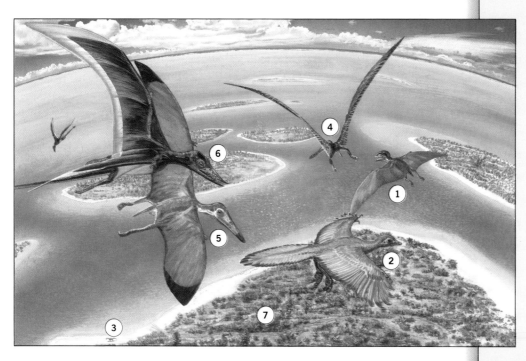

(Left) An underwater view of life in the sea at Eichstätt 145 million years ago. Above the surface of the water, pterosaurs fly overhead. In the distance is the mainland.

Solnhofen Quarry – Then
Pterosaurs and an early bird fly over coral islands and lagoons close to the mainland.
A *Rhamphorhynchus* and two species of *Pterodactylus* soar in search of fish to eat. The hawk-sized *Anurognathus* catches mayflies in flight, while a bird, *Archaeopteryx*, also hunts insects. Below, the islands are sandy and dotted with vegetation, such as low-growing club mosses, ginkgoes and bennettitaleans. A *Compsognathus* runs along the beach. The sea is rich in life, but the poisonous lower waters of the lagoons are as still as death.

Germany, Then and Now What is now central Europe was on the edge of the Atlantic and closer to the equator than it is today.

Globe shows the position of the continents now.

Solnhofen

FLYING DRAGONS

For aerial wildlife, the Late Jurassic Period was a time of great change. The earliest pterosaurs, the rhamphorhynchids (see page 14), dominated the sky in a variety of sizes. But the sleeker pterodactyls had emerged. Already some of them had grown to wingspans of 2.5 metres. Also at this time, the first known bird, *Archaeopteryx* (page 46) took wing. It evolved from dinosaurs.

Pterosaurs lived on all of the world's major land masses except Antarctica. Throughout the age of dinosaurs, even as some species of pterosaurs grew to 12-metre wingspans, all of them had a similar wing structure.

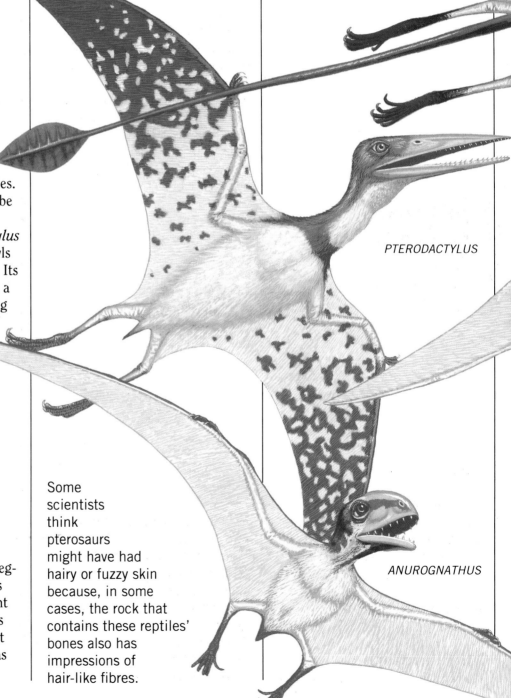

PTERODACTYLUS

ANUROGNATHUS

PTERODACTYLUS
Meaning of name: 'Wing-finger'
Order: Pterosauria
Size, Weight: 0.35 to 2.5 metres in wingspan, 1 to 10 kilos
Locations: Germany, France, England, Tanzania
Diet: Fish

Pterodactylus belonged to the pterodactyl group of flying reptiles. Some later pterodactyls grew to be enormous. They lasted until the end of dinosaur time. *Pterodactylus* was small, but like all pterodactyls it had a long neck and short tail. Its jaws were narrow and long, with a neater row of teeth for fish-eating than that of rhamphorhynchids.

ANUROGNATHUS
Meaning of name: 'Without tail jaw'
Order: Pterosauria
Size, Weight: 0.5 metres in wingspan, 1 kilo or less
Location: Germany
Diet: Insects

Anurognathus was a small rhamphorhynchid. Its head was short with a broad mouth and peg-like teeth, suggesting that it was not a fish-eater but that it caught insects in flight. *Anurognathus*'s short tail and light weight might have made this pterosaur agile as it chased fast-flying prey.

Some scientists think pterosaurs might have had hairy or fuzzy skin because, in some cases, the rock that contains these reptiles' bones also has impressions of hair-like fibres.

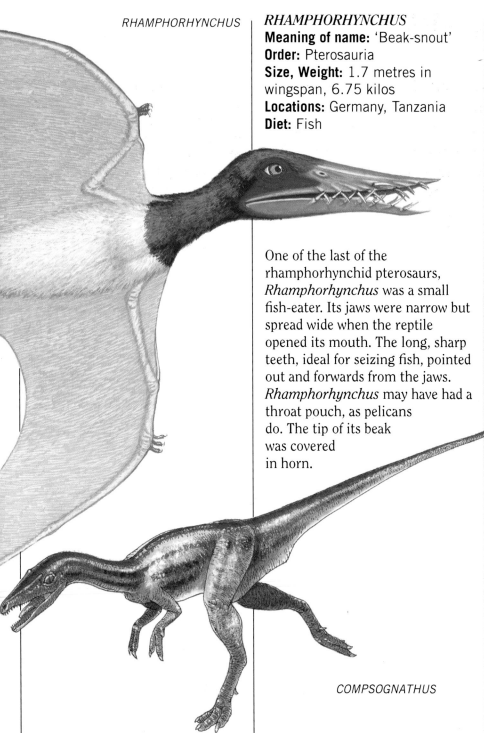

RHAMPHORHYNCHUS

RHAMPHORHYNCHUS
Meaning of name: 'Beak-snout'
Order: Pterosauria
Size, Weight: 1.7 metres in wingspan, 6.75 kilos
Locations: Germany, Tanzania
Diet: Fish

One of the last of the rhamphorhynchid pterosaurs, *Rhamphorhynchus* was a small fish-eater. Its jaws were narrow but spread wide when the reptile opened its mouth. The long, sharp teeth, ideal for seizing fish, pointed out and forwards from the jaws. *Rhamphorhynchus* may have had a throat pouch, as pelicans do. The tip of its beak was covered in horn.

COMPSOGNATHUS

COMPSOGNATHUS
Meaning of name: 'Elegant jaw'
Order: Saurischia
Size, Weight: 1 metre long, 2.75 to 3.5 kilos
Locations: Germany, France
Diet: Small vertebrates and insects

Fossils of this little meat-eater are very similar to those of the earliest known bird, *Archaeopteryx*, found at Eichstätt. *Compsognathus* is often named as the smallest dinosaur. But it was not. The first remains found of this meat-eater showed it was chicken-sized, but they belonged to a youngster. Full-grown, this animal was turkey-sized. Several plant-eating dinosaurs, including *Heterodontosaurus* and *Lesothosaurus*, were smaller.

SEA ANIMALS

Within the limestone of Solnhofen Quarry are sea creatures rarely preserved as fossils, such as squid with ten tentacles and jellyfish. Ammonites, sea lilies, sea urchins, starfish and brittle stars are preserved in detail.

JELLYFISH

Ray-finned fish like this one were common in Late Jurassic Europe. They were among the ancestors of modern bony fish.

Fish preserved in rock at Eichstätt

43

CORAL REEFS

Corals are tiny marine animals with soft bodies and tentacles. Many of them live today in huge colonies in shallow warm waters. Each of these animals produces an outer skeleton. Over time, many of these skeletons (one formed on top of another) can gradually build up to form an enormous rocky underwater ridge: a coral reef.

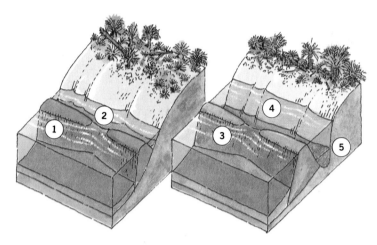

In Eichstätt, 145 million years ago, coral grew in the sun-warmed water offshore. This coral formed a barrier reef **(1)** and a lagoon **(2)** between land and sea. It is likely that rising sea levels caused the reef to grow higher **(3)** while water covered the shore **(4)**.

As the lagoon water evaporated, extremely salty water sank to the bottom **(5)**, which was protected from the waves. Storms brought in fresh seawater, which floated on top and also began to evaporate. Over time, the lagoon bottom became poisoned with salt.

One hundred and forty-five million years ago, Eichstätt was within the northern sub-tropical latitudes, and corals grew there. Today, coral reefs are among the richest habitats on Earth, with hundreds of different kinds of animals and plants. Some of the creatures, such as starfish, feed on the corals themselves. Others, like sharks, hunt the small fish that swim around the reefs and the shellfish that are attached to the coral.

At Eichstätt in the Late Jurassic, ammonites were among the most common animals in the lagoon. These were a group of now-extinct shelled animals. They lived in flat, tightly coiled shells that both protected the animals and probably contained air to help them float in the water. The nautilus of the Pacific Ocean today is similar to the ammonites in appearance and behaviour, but it is not closely related to it.

Coral reefs, like the Great Barrier Reef (left) off the coast of Australia, are found in tropical waters around the world. The Great Barrier Reef, which is nearly 2,000 kilometres long, is the world's largest.

In Late Jurassic Europe, a similar reef existed at Eichstätt. Today, this part of southern Germany is a high plateau near the Alps mountains.

A reef in the Philippines has up to four hundred different species of reef-building coral plus hundreds of other animals. The fossil record, although incomplete, indicates that the reef community of Eichstätt was also rich in species. As in coral reefs today, the corals that made up this ancient reef helped form the basis of a complex food web.

Coral communities look very different by day and by night. By day, fish swim about and feed, and invertebrates hide from predators. At night, the fish rest, and the corals put out their tentacles to feed. Many other invertebrates, including squid and sea urchins, emerge to feed.

Living in the sea were marine reptiles, fish and invertebrates (**1**). Corals and other tiny animals lived in the reefs (**2**). Behind the reefs, sponges and other simple life-forms grew in mounds (**3**). Other life survived in the lagoons' safe upper layer of water (**4**).

When a sick or injured animal sank to the bottom of one of these basins (**5**), it died in the poisoned lower waters. These deadly waters then prevented scavengers from destroying the body. In the calmest basins (**6**), dead animals lay undisturbed while they were covered by fine, soft sediment from the coral. Later, the land sank farther beneath the waters and the animals were fossilized.

FEATHERS IN THE ROCK

The most valuable and important fossil of all the treasures found in Eichstätt is *Archaeopteryx*, the earliest known bird. Only seven specimens of this 'missing link' have been uncovered. The first was found here in 1861, and it caused a sensation. For more than a century since then, scientists have argued over which animal was the ancestor of this bird.

Archaeopteryx had feathers and a beak, as birds do. But it was unlike any modern bird in several ways. Its beak held many small pointed teeth. Its tail was long and bony, unlike a modern bird's. Its wings had three fingers with claws. Only one living bird, the hoatzin, has wing claws. Scientists now think *Archaeopteryx* descended from meat-eating dinosaurs like *Compsognathus*, which had a similar anatomy but no feathers.

The relative sizes of *Compsognathus* and *Archaeopteryx*. As with all prehistoric creatures, we do not know their real colours. Some artists show *Archaeopteryx* with colourful feathers, others with drab-coloured feathers.

Compsognathus

Archaeopteryx

Archaeopteryx* and *Compsognathus skeletons are similar. 'Wishbones' (collarbones formerly thought to be typical only of birds) have been found on some meat-eating dinosaurs.

This, the finest *Archaeopteryx* specimen, was discovered in Eichstätt in 1877. Faint impressions of feathers can be seen on the wings, tail and body. This fossil is displayed in the Museum of Natural History in Berlin, Germany. Some scientists believe that, despite its feathers, *Archaeopteryx* could not fly.

ARCHAEOPTERYX FOSSILIZES

An *Archaeopteryx* flies low over the ancient Solnhofen Quarry site **(1)**, looking for flying insects to eat. Along the coast, the lagoon waters, usually still, are whipped into waves by storm winds.

A gust catches the bird's outstretched wings and knocks the creature from the sky into the lagoon **(2)**. The *Archaeopteryx* cannot swim and its feathers are too laden with water for the animal to fly. It tries to paddle to the shore, but without success.

The still and poisonous Eichstätt lagoon of the Late Jurassic Period captured plants and animals that lived and died along its surface or were washed into it by rain, waves or winds.

The creatures fell to the bottom of the lagoon. There, the bodies immediately left impressions in the soft lime powder that had settled as it flaked off the dead coral of the reef. Undisturbed for centuries, the animals' skeletons were also left intact. The result was a series of astonishing fossils. Many bones were preserved in their proper places within the outlines of the animals' soft tissues. Also, those tissues – such as flesh, scales and feathers – had left impressions in the rock. At Solnhofen Quarry, scientists have a record of insects, pterosaurs, birds and marine creatures that are not usually fossilized.

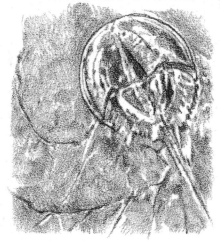

Footprints of a horseshoe crab preserved in rock. In the deadly water of the lagoon, the crab wandered in circles as if it were groggy before it died.

Archaeopteryx soon drowns in the choppy, shallow water. The dead bird quickly sinks to the still bottom of the lagoon **(3)** and falls on its back into the soft mud, leaving an imprint of its feathers on the sea floor **(4)**.

Within weeks, the flesh and feathers rot away, but the bones remain in place. Meanwhile, tiny particles of lime from the dead coral of the reef continue to drift through the water. This lime settles over the *Archaeopteryx*.

Over thousands of years the particles are compressed to stone, preserving the ancient bird inside. About 145 million years later, quarry workers chop out slabs of the limestone. The stone separates easily, especially in places where fossils have interrupted the formation of stone. A worker splits one block of stone and uncovers the impression of a nearly complete *Archaeopteryx* (see page 46).

INDEX